I WONDER
HOW TIRES ARE MADE

Neil Curtis and Peter Greenland

Lerner Publications Company • Minneapolis

This edition published 1992
by Lerner Publications Company
241 First Avenue North
Minneapolis, Minnesota 55401 USA

Original edition published in 1990 by Heinemann Educational
Books Ltd., Halley Court, Jordan Hill, Oxford OX28EJ England
Copyright © 1990 by Heinemann Educational Books Ltd.

Library of Congress Cataloging-in-Publication Data

Curtis, Neil.
  How tires are made / Neil Curtis and Peter Greenland.
     p.   cm. — (I wonder)
  Originally published: Oxford, England : Heinemann
Educational Books, 1990.
  Summary: Describes how tires are made, illustrating the
process that begins on a rubber tree plantation and ends at
a factory.
  ISBN 0-8225-2377-9
  1. Tires, Rubber—Juvenile literature. 2. Rubber—Juvenile
literature. [1. Tires, Rubber. 2. Rubber.] I. Greenland, Peter.
II. Title. III. Series: Curtis, Neil. I wonder.
  TS1912.C87   1992
  678′.32—dc20   91-24846
                                                        CIP
                                                        AC

Manufactured in the United States of America.

1 2 3 4 5 6 7 8 9 10 01 00 99 98 97 96 95 94 93 92

With good tires, this bus can ride smoothly,
even on bumpy roads.
Tires also keep the bus from skidding
when it stops.

Tires are made of rubber.
Some rubber is made from
a mixture of chemicals.
Other kinds of rubber come from a special tree.

Rubber trees grow wild in South American jungles, and they grow on plantations in Southeast Asia. The juice inside the trees is a watery rubber.

To collect the juice, a worker makes a cut
in the bark of a rubber tree.
The milky white liquid, called latex,
runs into a cup.

Each worker on a plantation cuts many trees.
A few hours later, the workers come back
to see if the cups are full.

The workers pour the latex from the cups
into barrels.
Then they carry the heavy barrels
to the plantation's rubber factory.

At the factory, the latex is poured into a tank
filled with acid.
The acid separates the water from the latex.

Workers roll the lumps of pure rubber
into sheets.

Next the sheets of rubber
are hung in a smokehouse.
Smoke makes the rubber tougher.

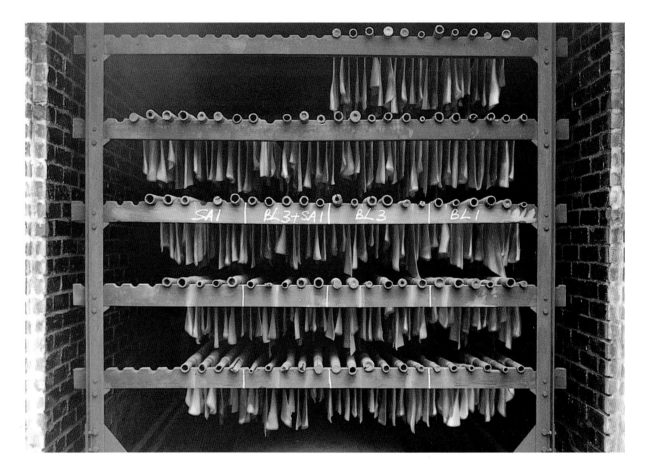

Now the rubber is ready to go to
a factory that makes tires.

At the tire factory, the rubber from the plantation is mixed with rubber made from chemicals. Mixers and grinders crunch the two kinds of rubber together.

Then the rubber goes into a machine with rollers.
The rollers press the rubber into sheets.

The sheets of rubber are almost ready to use.
But first they must be made stronger.

Cords made of steel or nylon are coated with rubber.

The cords are pressed into the rubber sheets
to make the sheets tougher.
Now the rubber can be used to build a tire.

A tire is built around a form called a drum.
A worker wraps the drum with layers of rubber
and cloth, and with loops of strong wire.

The tire is taken off the drum.

Next a tread is made for the tire.
The tread is the part of the tire that
touches the road.

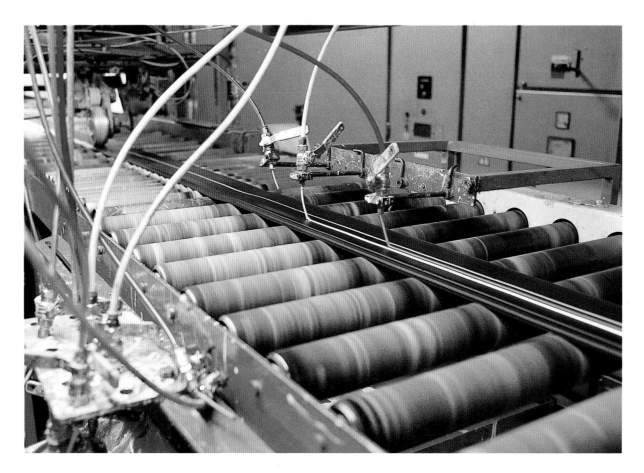

A different machine makes the tread.

Another worker shapes the tread around the tire.

Then the tire goes into a machine that
heats it and makes the rubber hard.

This machine also stamps a pattern
into the tire's tread.

An inspector checks the finished tire.

We use tires on our bicycles,
trucks, tractors, and cars.
Tires take us from place to place
in all kinds of weather.